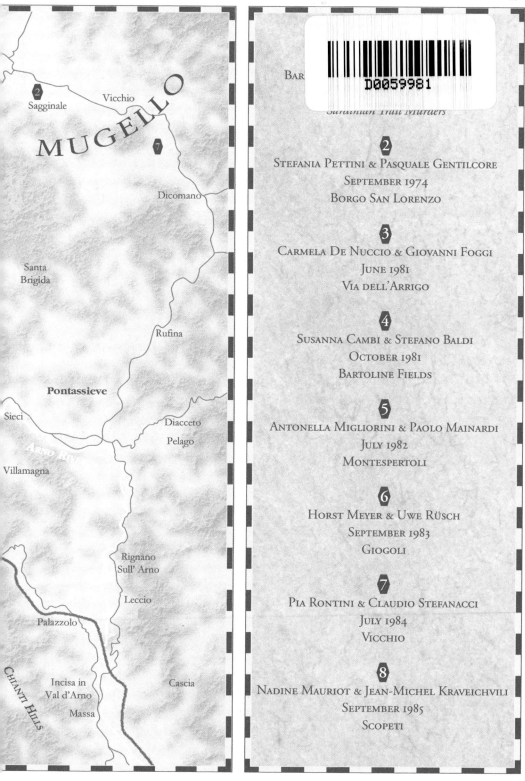

CONCORD

MUGELLO

Sagginale

2

Vicchio

7

Dicomano

Santa
Brigida

Rufina

Pontassieve

Sieci

Diacceto

Pelago

ARNO RIVER

Villamagna

Rignano
Sull' Arno

Leccio

Palazzolo

CHIANTI HILLS

Incisa in
Val d'Arno

Massa

Cascia

BAR

Sardinian Trail Murders

2

STEFANIA PETTINI & PASQUALE GENTILCORE
SEPTEMBER 1974
BORGO SAN LORENZO

3

CARMELA DE NUCCIO & GIOVANNI FOGGI
JUNE 1981
VIA DELL'ARRIGO

4

SUSANNA CAMBI & STEFANO BALDI
OCTOBER 1981
BARTOLINE FIELDS

5

ANTONELLA MIGLIORINI & PAOLO MAINARDI
JULY 1982
MONTESPERTOLI

6

HORST MEYER & UWE RÜSCH
SEPTEMBER 1983
GIOGOLI

7

PIA RONTINI & CLAUDIO STEFANACCI
JULY 1984
VICCHIO

8

NADINE MAURIOT & JEAN-MICHEL KRAVEICHVILI
SEPTEMBER 1985
SCOPETI

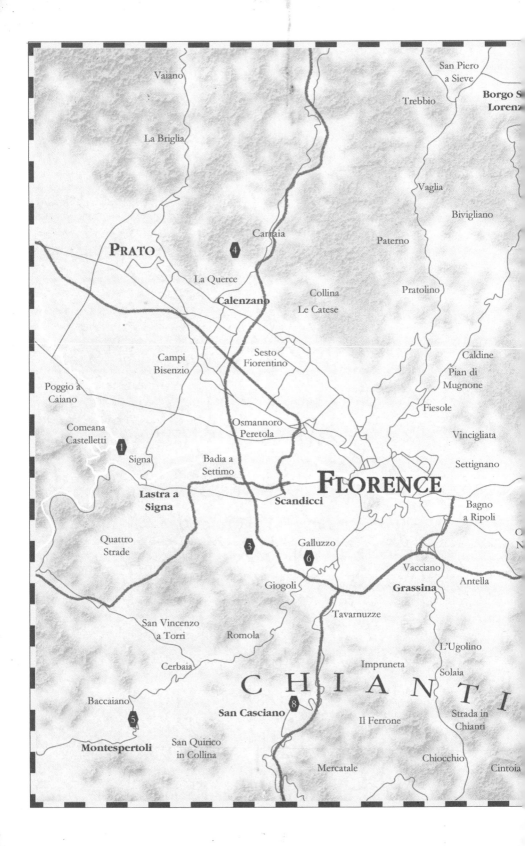

COMMITTEE ON EVALUATING CLINICAL APPLICATIONS OF TELEMEDICINE

JOHN R. BALL, M.D., J.D.,* *Chair,* President and CEO, Pennsylvania Hospital, Philadelphia

MICKEY S. EISENBERG, M.D., Ph.D.,* Director, Emergency Medicine Service, University of Washington Medical Center, Seattle

MELVYN GREBERMAN, M.D., M.P.H., Associate Director for Medical Affairs Division of Small Manufacturers Assistance, Food and Drug Administration, U.S. Department of Health and Human Services, Rockville, Maryland

MICHAEL HATTWICK, M.D., President, Woodburn Internal Medicine Associates, Annandale, Virginia

SUSAN D. HORN, Ph.D., Senior Scientist, Institute for Clinical Outcomes Research, Salt Lake City, Utah

PETER O. KOHLER, M.D.,* President, Oregon Health Sciences University, Portland

NINA W. MATHESON, M.L.,* Director Emerita, William H. Welch Library, Professor of Medical Information, Johns Hopkins University, Baltimore, Maryland

DAVID B. NASH, M.D., Director of Health Policy and Clinical Outcomes, Thomas Jefferson University Hospital, Philadelphia

JUDITH OZBOLT, Ph.D., R.N., Professor, University of Virginia School of Nursing, Charlottesville, Virginia

JAMES S. ROBERTS, M.D., Senior Vice President, Clinical Leadership, VHA, Inc., Irving, Texas

JAY H. SANDERS, M.D., Director of Telemedicine Center, Professor of Medicine and Surgery, Medical College of Georgia, Augusta

JOHN C. SCOTT, M.S., President, Center for Public Service Communications, Arlington, Virginia

JANE E. SISK, Ph.D., Professor, Division of Health Policy and Management, Columbia University School of Public Health, New York

---

* Member, Institute of Medicine.

PAUL C. TANG, M.D., Associate Professor of Medicine, Northwestern University Medical School, and Medical Director, Information Systems, Northwestern Memorial Hospital, Chicago

ERIC TANGALOS, M.D., Associate Professor of Medicine, Mayo Clinic, Rochester, Minnesota

Technical Advisory Panel to the Committee

RASHID L. BASHSHUR, Ph.D., Professor, Department of Health Management and Policy, School of Public Health, The University of Michigan, Ann Arbor

DOUGLAS D. BRADHAM, Dr.P.H.,** Associate Professor, Bowman Gray School of Medicine, Department of Public Health Sciences, Section on Social Sciences and Health Policy, Wake Forest University, Winston-Salem, North Carolina

LINDA H. BRINK, Ph.D., Chair, U.S. Department of Defense Testbed Telemedicine Evaluation Working Group, U.S. Army Medical Research and Materiel Command, Walter Reed Army Medical Center, Washington, D.C.

JIM GRIGSBY, Ph.D., Associate Professor, University of Colorado Health Sciences Center, and Senior Researcher, Centers for Health Policy and Health Services Research, Denver

CAROLE L. MINTZER, M.P.A., Senior Finance Analyst, Office of Rural Health Policy, Rockville, Maryland

DOUGLAS A. PEREDNIA, M.D., Director, Telemedicine Research Center and Oregon State Health Sciences University Advanced Telemedicine Research Group, Portland

Study Staff

MARILYN J. FIELD, Ph.D., Study Director
KARLA R. SAUNDERS, Administrative Assistant
ELINOR C. GRAY, Research Assistant

**As of July 1996, Director, Section on Medical Outcomes and Policy Analysis, and Associate Professor, University of Maryland School of Medicine, Department of Medicine, Division of Gerontology, Baltimore, Maryland.

Acknowledgments

Many individuals and groups assisted the study committee and staff in the development of this report. We particularly benefited from the experience and wisdom of the Technical Advisory Panel (listed after the committee), both as a group and as individuals.

A number of those involved with the federal Joint Working Group on Telemedicine provided information and advice throughout the project. Dena Puskin, Sc.D., chair of the working group and Deputy Director of the Office of Rural Health Policy, was unfailingly helpful with her time and insights. Linda Brink, Ph.D., Chair of the Department of Defense Telemedicine Evaluation Working Group, contributed generously from her evaluation experience. She also arranged an on-site visit to the telemedicine center at Walter Reed Army Medical Center and provided periodic updates on the military's development of evaluation tools and processes.

Michael Ackerman, Ph.D., was a pleasure to work with, both as project officer for this study for the National Library of Medicine (NLM) and as a participant in many key information infrastructure activities. Donald Lindberg, M.D., Director of the NLM and Betsy Humphreys, M.L.S., Deputy Associate Director of NLM Library Operations provided important direction early in planning the study. William England, Ph.D., the project officer from the Health Care Financing Administration, was also very helpful. From the early days of the study, Colonel Joan Zajtchuk and Brigadier General Russ Zajtchuk of the U.S. Army provided information and other assistance, including invitations to several military telemedicine meetings.

Committee members and staff met with representatives of many organizations and visited several telemedicine projects. Joseph Gitlin, D.P.H., graciously helped to organize our visit to the University of Maryland Medical System and the Baltimore Veterans Affairs Medical Center (VAMC). (He also worked with Melvyn Greberman, a committee member, to arrange discussions with participants at annual meetings of the Radiological Society of North America and the Society for Computer Applications in Radiology.) In Baltimore, we especially appreciated the time Eliot Siegel, M.D., of the VAMC spent with us, providing a very helpful review of their decision to adopt filmless radiology and their internal assessments of the effects on productivity. Richard Alcorta, M.D., and Gene Bidun of the Maryland Institute of Emergency Medical Services System gave us an overview and tour of the organizaton's headquarters. Deborah Finkelsen, Stephen Schimpff, M.D., Colin MacKenzie, M.D., and Robert Allman, M.D., of the University of Maryland contributed to our education about their activities.

Douglas Perednia, M.D., arranged for the committee to hear from him, Dan Filiburti, Nancy Brown, M.L.S., Tamara Hayes, Ph.D., Jim Wallace, and others about the activities of the Telemedicine Research Center and the research being undertaken at Oregon Health Sciences University. He also arranged for a "televisit" with Catherine Britain of RODEO NET, which provided an unplanned opportunity to experience some of the technical problems that can complicate interactive audio-video conferencing. Peter Kohler, M.D. (a committee member), and Carol Reinmiller kindly enabled the committee to get a broader view of telemedicine in Oregon by arranging meetings with those involved with state telecommunications policy and with educational uses of telemedicine. Participants included Donald Girard, M.D., Paula McNeil, R.N., Lesley Hallick, Ph.D., James Walker, James Elert, John Saultz, M.D., Mark Dodson, Deana Molinari, R.N., M.S.N., and Hersch Crawford.

At the University of Washington, Tara Cannava, M.H.A., arranged a discussion with those evaluating the WAMI Rural Telemedicine Network including Gary Hart, M.D., Peter House, M.H.A.,

Mike Pirani, Ph.D., and Peter West, M.D. Alan Rowberg, M.D., demonstrated some of the technical and practical issues in integrating digital radiology with traditional film-based operations in radiology departments, emergency departments, and intensive care units.

Chris Barnard, M.D., Medical Director of the Stanford Telemedicine Program, showed us the medical center side of some of the University's telemedicine activities and also took us to two of their "remote" sites. Rodney Hawkins, M.P.A., Purna Prasad, M.S., Linda Cook, R.N., Rick Kong, Gerry Shebar provided insights into the strategic, business, engineering, and management aspects of their program. At the Lytton Gardens Health Care Center, we met with Vera Goupille, M.P.H., Peter Pompei, M.D., and Linda Hibbs, R.N., M.P.A. At Drew Health Foundation, we met with administrator Manfred Hayes, M.B.A., Dana Knoll, M.B.A., Bertha Price, L.V.N., and others. An attempt to arrange a video link with the San Jose Medical Group failed because severe storms disrupted telephone communication in the Bay Area, but this experience, again, was instructional.

William Goodall, M.D., of Allina Health System; Ed Hinman, M.D., of Total Healthcare; and John Santa, M.D., Joanne Zamorra, and Eric Livingston, all of Blue Cross/Blue Shield of Oregon talked with us about telemedicine in different kinds of managed care environments. Robert Thompson, M.D., invited staff to participate in a meeting of the American College of Radiology and National Electrical Manufacturers Association that illuminated some of the difficulties of building on and extending their experience in developing the DICOM standards for radiology.

Francoise Gilbert, J.D., of Altheimer & Gray, Chicago, and Leo J. Whelan, J.D., Legal Counsel, for Mayo Clinic, Rochester, Minnesota, reviewed drafts of the policy chapter, which greatly benefited from their suggestions (although they bear no responsibility for any errors). In addition to helping draft a background paper for the committee, Neil Neuberger provided numerous information resources and contacts. Among others who were helpful in a variety of ways were Richard Bakalar, M.D., U.S. Navy; Roger Shannon, M.D., Veterans Health Administration; Gloria Jones of East Carolina University; Donna Farley, M.H.A., now of the Rand Organization; Suzanne Tichenor of the Council on Competitiveness; Alice Meyer at md/tv; Barry Rome at VTEL; Sharon Cauchi of Telemedicine and Telehealth Networks; and Ace Allen, M.D., of Telemedicine Today.

Staff within the Institute of Medicine provided assistance in many different ways. Some of those we especially thank include Claudia Carl, Nina Spruill, Mary Lee Schneiders, Mike Edington, Donna Thompson, Richard Julian, and Molla Donaldson. At the Computer Sciences and Telecommunications Board of the National Research Council, first Louise Arnheim and then Jerry Sheehan were the staff liaisons for this project.

Contents

TABLES, FIGURES, AND BOXES

Tables

Figures

Boxes

Telemedicine

Summary

For more than 30 years, clinicians, health services researchers, and others have been investigating the use of advanced telecommunications and information technologies to improve health care. At the intersection of many of these efforts lies telemedicine—a combination of innovative and mainstream technologies. As defined here, telemedicine is *the use of electronic information and communications technologies to provide and support health care when distance separates the participants.*

Telemedicine has a variety of applications in patient care, education, research, administration, and public health. Some uses such as emergency calls to 911 numbers using ordinary telephones are so commonplace that they are often overlooked as examples of distance medicine. Other applications such as telesurgery involve exotic technologies and procedures that are still in the experimental stage. The use of interactive video for such varied purposes as psychiatric consultations and home monitoring of patients attracts much attention and news coverage, although such applications are far from routine in everyday medical practice.

For many decisionmakers, the case for new or continued investment in telemedicine remains incomplete, particularly given the competition for resources in an era of budgetary retrenchment in health care and government. Most clinical applications of telemedicine

1

have not been subjected to systematic comparative studies that assess their effects on the quality, accessibility, or cost of health care. Although telemedicine is hardly unique among health care services in lacking evidence of its effectiveness, the increasing demand for such evidence by health plans, patients, clinicians, and policymakers challenges advocates of clinical telemedicine to undertake more and better evaluations of its practicality, value, and affordability.

In response to the scarcity of sound evaluations, the National Library of Medicine (NLM) asked the Institute of Medicine (IOM) to develop a broad framework for evaluating clinical telemedicine. This report, developed by a 15-member committee of the IOM, presents that framework, which focuses on telemedicine's effects on the quality, accessibility, cost, and acceptability of health care. The objective is to encourage evaluations that will guide policymakers, reassure patients and clinicians, inform health plan managers, and help those who have invested in telemedicine to identify shortcomings and improve their programs. This report is aimed primarily at these policymakers, clinicians, patients, and managers, but it is also intended to provide context and support for researchers with an interest in evaluating information and communications technologies.

TELEMEDICINE PAST AND PRESENT

Historically, access concerns have driven much of the work to develop clinical telemedicine. Early applications often focused on remote populations scattered across mountainous areas, islands, open plains, and arctic regions where medical specialists and sometimes primary care practitioners were not easily reached. Most of the telemedicine projects from the 1960s through the early 1980s failed, however, to survive the end of grant funding or trial financing. Telecommunications costs tended to be high, and the technologies were awkward to use. Few projects appeared to be guided by a business plan or an appreciation of the project features and results necessary for a sustainable program.

Recently, another wave of interest in telemedicine has prompted a range of new activities. Costs have dropped for many of the information and communications technologies supporting telemedicine, and the developing National Information Infrastructure (NII) is making these technologies more commonplace and more easily used.

Teleradiology appears to be the most common application, in part because Medicare and other payers reimburse for radiology consultations without demanding the face-to-face relationship required for most other consultations.

With the nation's health care system undergoing profound changes and experiencing relentless financial pressures, telemedicine is being investigated for its utility in urban as well as rural settings. To the extent that telemedicine offers a mechanism for centralizing specialists and supporting primary care clinicians, managed care plans may find certain applications efficient and attractive in the cities and suburbs where their patients are concentrated. Some academic medical centers and other organizations, faced with reduced revenues and even exclusion from local managed care networks, are exploring telemedicine as they seek to develop new regional, national, and international markets for their highly specialized clinicians. In these contexts, telemedicine has the potential to radically reshape health care in both positive and negative ways and to fundamentally alter the personal face-to-face relationship that has been the model for medical care for generations.

Despite recent growth, obstacles to widespread use of clinical telemedicine persist. For example, although many groups are working to develop hardware and software standards, it remains frustrating and difficult to put together systems in which the components operate predictably and smoothly together, work in different settings without extensive adaptation, and accommodate replacement components. Technical systems still may be poorly adapted to the human infrastructure of health care, that is, the work environment, needs, and preferences of clinicians, patients, and other decision-makers. Moreover, sustainable telemedicine programs require attention to organizational business objectives and strategic plans that is not always evident in current applications.

In a period characterized by increased competition, structural realignments, and surpluses of some categories of health professionals, clinicians may see telemedicine as an economic threat. Even though interstate telemedicine is not a priority for many users or potential users, jurisdictional issues relating to professional licensure and medical liability are generating considerable controversy. As computer-based patient information systems and databases have proliferated, the relative weakness of state and federal policies to protect the privacy and confidentiality of personal medical information has stimulated legislative reform proposals but no action to date.

CHALLENGES IN EVALUATING CLINICAL TELEMEDICINE

Major challenges confront those evaluating clinical applications of telemedicine. These difficulties also characterize many other applications of advanced technologies, and, thus, they are not unique to telemedicine. Nonetheless, the combination of challenges is formidable. They include

• *the rapid advance of information and telecommunications technologies*, which exposes systematic and often expensive evaluations to obsolescence as key hardware and software components of telemedicine applications move from state of the art to outmoded;
• *a complex and often unwieldy technical infrastructure*, which may yield disappointing evaluations until it becomes more ubiquitous and user-friendly;
• *a diverse and sometimes dazzling array of telemedicine technologies and uses* that may distract managers and evaluators from the task of identifying practical, affordable, and sustainable ways to achieve defined quality, access, or cost objectives; and
• *the unusual level of cooperation that medicine at a distance often demands of independent institutions and individuals* whose reluctance to participate may preclude the kinds of comparisons and the volume of cases needed for strong evaluations.

In addition, several more general challenges may complicate evaluations of clinical telemedicine. One is the restructuring of the nation's health care delivery system, which has brought with it shifts in institutional missions and priorities related to patient care, education, and research. A second is the growth of investor-owned enterprises that are not much inclined to allocate resources for purposes such as clinical research that do not add to corporate profits. At the state and federal level, policymakers are cutting budgets and may be reluctant to shift even modest resources from the core activities of grant programs to support evaluations of their actual consequences.

Fortunately, a number of government and private organizations have recognized the need for more systematic evaluation of tele-medicine. This report draws on this work as well as on the contributions of individual researchers who are also working to improve the methods and strengthen the evidence base for telemedicine.

A FRAMEWORK FOR EVALUATION

In most respects, better evaluations of clinical telemedicine will depend on careful attention to evaluation concepts and methods that form the well-established foundation of health services research and evaluation research generally. The framework presented in this report has four components: basic principles, a careful planning process, key evaluation elements, and fundamental evaluation questions. The principles that guided the development of the framework call for telemedicine evaluations to be

• treated as an integral part of program design, implementation, and redesign;

• viewed as a cumulative and forward-looking process for building useful knowledge for decisionmakers rather than as an isolated research exercise;

• designed to compare the benefits and costs of telemedicine with those of current practice; and

• focused on identifying practical and economical ways to achieve desired results rather than investigating the most exciting or advanced telemedicine options.

In conjunction with these principles, the evaluation framework developed by this study (Box S.1) constitutes a base for strengthening individual evaluations of telemedicine and encouraging the coordination of evaluation strategies across projects and organizations, when possible. The framework highlights the importance of both delineating how technical, clinical, and administrative processes are intended to work *and* determining how they actually are implemented. This is crucial if evaluators who find disappointing or unexpected results are (a) to distinguish the failure of an application from the failure of an application to be implemented as intended and (b) to provide guidance to decisionmakers considering whether to adopt, substantially redesign, or discontinue telemedicine programs.

The fast pace of change and other uncertainties surrounding telemedicine applications argue strongly for an evaluation plan to

Box S.1
Elements of an Evaluation Plan

Project description and research question(s): the application or program to be evaluated and the basic questions to be answered by the evaluation.

Strategic objectives: how the project is intended to serve the sponsor or parent organization's purposes.

Clinical objectives: how the telemedicine project is intended to affect individual or population health by changing the quality, accessibility, or cost of care.

Business plan or project management plan: a formal statement of how the evaluation will help decisionmakers judge whether and when the application will be a financially and otherwise sustainable enterprise or, less formally, what the project's management, work plan, schedule, and budget will be.

Level and perspective of evaluation: whether the focus of the research question(s) and objectives is clinical, institutional, societal, or some combination.

Research design and analysis plan: the strategy and steps for developing valid comparative information and analyzing it.

Experimental and comparison groups: characteristics of (a) the group or groups that will be involved in testing the target telemedicine application and (b) the group or groups that will receive alternative services for purposes of comparison.

Technical, clinical, and administrative processes: as planned and actually implemented, the communications and information systems, the methods for providing medical care, and the supportive organizational processes.

Measurable outcomes: the variables and the data to be collected to determine whether the project is meeting its clinical and strategic objectives.

Sensitivity analysis: the inclusion of techniques to assess to what extent conclusions may change if assumptions or values of key variables changed.

Documentation: the explicit reporting of the methods employed in the evaluation and the findings so that others can determine how the results were established.

include sensitivity analyses that explore to what extent conclusions may change if values of key variables or assumptions change. Such analyses are appropriately keyed to a business plan that explicitly states how the evaluation will provide information to help decisionmakers determine whether a telemedicine application is useful, consistent with their goals and objectives, and sustainable beyond the evaluation phase.

To build both on this framework and on past initiatives, the committee encourages federal agencies to strengthen provisions for evaluating demonstration projects and other telemedicine activities and to support innovative research strategies and methods development. Given the relative sparsity of evaluations of telemedicine, the committee also urges those sponsoring and funding a number of different projects to consider how their project evaluations might be designed to reinforce and supplement each other despite differences in the objectives, applications, and other characteristics of the projects. The efforts of the federal Joint Working Group on Telemedicine are constructive steps in this direction.

In the private sector, the committee likewise encourages organizations considering telemedicine to build evaluation into their program plans. Decisionmakers can also demand from vendors more complete and relevant documentation of costs and promised benefits.

Finally, because the evaluation literature in telemedicine is weighted toward nonexperimental studies, the report particularly encourages researchers and funding organizations to look beyond nonexperimental designs to more rigorous experimental and quasi-experimental designs. The latter attempts to control some important threats to validity through statistical adjustments and other means when random assignment of participants, homogeneous populations, or strict treatment protocols are not feasible. Sophisticated computer-based patient information systems are gradually making such designs more practical and robust. Peer-reviewed publications can also play a role by moving toward standards for systematic reporting of evaluation methods and results.

BASIC EVALUATION QUESTIONS

Clinical applications of telemedicine are marked by diversity. They differ in the medical problems addressed, the evidence base for decisionmaking, the personnel and settings of care involved, the diagnostic and therapeutic strategies employed, and the organizational and cost implications of these strategies. Given the large number of possible quality, access, cost, and acceptability measures for different clinical applications of telemedicine and the difficulty of stipulating many of them in abstract form, this study did not focus on application-specific measures and criteria.

Instead, to guide the selection of evaluation criteria or measures for particular evaluation projects, it proposed broadly relevant questions about the quality, accessibility, cost, and acceptability of telemedicine services. *Quality* is the degree to which health care services for individuals and populations increase the likelihood of desired health outcomes and are consistent with current professional knowledge. *Access* refers to the timely receipt of appropriate care (or, more informally, the right care at the right time without undue burden). The *cost* of care is the economic value of resource use associated with the pursuit of defined objectives or outcomes. *Acceptability* refers to the degree to which patients, clinicians, or others are satisfied with a service or willing to use it. In some telemedicine evaluations, patient satisfaction data appear to be the only patient-level data collected, a focus that the committee considers too limiting.

Box S.2 presents the basic categories of evaluation questions identified by the committee, and the appendix to this summary lists more specific questions in each category. Although the questions present the concepts of quality, access, cost, and acceptability in sequence, their interactions and interrelationships also warrant evaluation. More generally, the questions should be considered in the context of the overall evaluation framework. That is, relevant patient and organizational characteristics should be identified and considered as they might affect results. The actual as well as the planned technical and clinical processes should be recorded. The fit between the project objectives and results and the sponsoring organization's purposes or strategic plan also needs to be factored into the plan for analysis and the interpretation of results.

For some evaluation results, the findings will strongly suggest certain decisions. For example, if a telemedicine application is more costly than the alternative and performs less well (e.g., produces fewer health benefits), it should not be adopted. Likewise, if the application is more costly and performs as well, it should not be adopted. In contrast, if the telemedicine application is less costly but performs better than the alternative or if it is less costly and performs as well, it should be considered. Results are sometimes more equivocal and decisions more difficult. For example, if a telemedicine

---

Box S.2
Categories of Evaluation Questions for Comparing
Telemedicine to Alternative Health Services

1. What were the effects of the application on the clinical process of care compared to the alternative(s)?
2. What were the effects of the application on patient status or health outcomes compared to the alternative(s)?
3. What were the effects of the application on access compared to the alternative(s)?
4. What were the costs of the application for patients, private or public payers, providers, and other affected parties compared to the alternative(s)?
5. How did patients, clinicians, and other relevant parties view the application and were they satisfied with the application compared to the alternative(s)?

NOTE: Each question assumes that results will be analyzed controlling for or taking into account severity of illness, comorbidities, demographic characteristics, and other relevant factors.

---

application is more costly and performs better than the alternative, are the benefits gained worth the extra costs? If an alternative is less costly and performs less well, are the savings worth the health benefits foregone?

Some telemedicine evaluations will focus less on individual patients than on populations, including but not limited to those enrolled in managed care plans. Analyses may consider outcomes for an entire patient population or may concentrate on outcomes for the least healthy or most vulnerable groups in a population (e.g., elderly individuals, migrant workers). In addition, because telemedicine programs may also serve educational and administrative as well as clinical objectives, evaluations may reasonably seek to assess program effects in these areas. Broader community effects may also be considered. For example, although improved access to health care for rural populations has been an important objective of many telemedicine projects, policymakers may also be interested in the effects of telemedicine on the survival of rural health care providers and the implications of such effects on the economic health of rural areas including their ability to attract or maintain business, educational, and other resources.

CONCLUSION

Special challenges notwithstanding, more rigorous and systematic evaluation is as necessary for telemedicine as it is for other health care technologies. Decisionmakers still do not have good enough information comparing the effects of telemedicine applications to alternative health care strategies. They also lack good analyses of the infrastructure implications and financial requirements for sustaining telemedicine past an initial "test of concept" period.

Although individual research approaches will vary, the evaluation and implementation of telemedicine projects will benefit by the more consistent adoption of sound evaluation principles and methods. They will also benefit from the lessons learned in implementing computer-based patient records and integrated patient information systems, an undertaking that remains dauntingly difficult, even after 25 years of groundwork. These difficulties suggest the importance of persistence and realism for those working to demonstrate telemedicine's promise.

For some applications of telemedicine, more rigorous evaluations will make claims of their value more credible and will encourage their more widespread use. For other applications, better evaluation may discourage adoption, at least until technologies or infrastructures improve or other circumstances change. This is to be expected. The purpose of evaluation—and the purpose of this report—is not to endorse telemedicine but to endorse the development and use of good information for decisionmaking. The evaluation framework presented here is offered in that spirit.

APPENDIX:
QUESTIONS ABOUT THE QUALITY, ACCESSIBILITY, COST, AND ACCEPTABILITY OF TELEMEDICINE

Evaluating Quality of Care and Health Outcomes

What were the effects of the telemedicine application on the clinical process of care compared to the alternative(s)?

Was the application associated with differences in the use of health services (e.g., office visits, emergency transfers, diagnostic tests, length of hospital stay)?

Was the application associated with differences in appropriateness of services (e.g., underuse of clearly beneficial care)?

Was the application associated with differences in the quality, amount, or type of information available to clinicians or patients?

Was the application associated with differences in patients' knowledge of their health status, their understanding of the care options, or their compliance with care regimens?

Was the application associated with differences in diagnostic accuracy or timeliness, patient management decisions, or technical performance?

Was the application associated with differences in the interpersonal aspects of care?

What were the effects of the telemedicine application on immediate, intermediate, or long-term health outcomes compared to the alternative(s)?

Was the application associated with differences in physical signs or symptoms?

Was the application associated with differences in morbidity or mortality?

Was the application associated with a difference in physical, mental, or social and role functioning?

Was the application associated with differences in health-related behaviors (e.g., compliance with treatment regimens)?

Was the application associated with differences in patients' satisfaction with their care or patients' perceptions about the quality or acceptability of the care they received?

Evaluating Access to Care

Did telemedicine affect the use of services or the level or appropriateness of care compared to the alternative(s)?

What was the utilization of telemedicine services before, during, and after the study period for target population and clinical problem(s)?

When offered the option of a telemedicine service, how often did patients

- accept or refuse an initial service or fail to keep an appointment?
- accept or refuse a subsequent service or fail to keep an appointment?

What was the utilization of specified alternative services before, during, and after the study period for the target population and clinical problem(s)?

- consultants traveling to distant sites
- patients traveling to distant consultants
- consultation by mail or courier
- transfers to other facilities
- self-care

Was the telemedicine application associated with a difference in overall utilization (e.g., number of services or rate) or indicators of appropriateness of care for

- specialty care
- primary care
- transport services
- services associated with lack of timely care?

Did the application affect the timeliness of care or the burden of obtaining care compared to the alternative(s)?

Was there a difference in the

- timing of care
- appointment waiting times for referrals?

What were patient attitudes about the

- timeliness of care
- burden of obtaining care
- appropriateness of care?

What were the attitudes of attending and consulting physicians and other personnel about the

- timeliness of care
- burden of providing care
- appropriateness of care?

Evaluating Health Care Costs and Cost-Effectiveness

What were the costs of the telemedicine application for participating health care providers or health plans compared to the alternative(s)?

Was an application associated with differences in attending clinicians' costs for personnel, equipment, supplies, administrative services, travel, or other items? Was an application associated with differences in revenues or productivity? What was the net effect?

Was an application associated with differences in consulting clinicians' or consulting organizations' costs for personnel, equipment, supplies, space, administrative services, travel, or other items? Was an application associated with differences in revenues or productivity? What was the net effect?

Was an application associated with differences in the cost per service, per episode of illness, or per member (health plan enrollee, capitated lives) per month?

What were the costs of the telemedicine application for patients and families compared to the alternative(s)?

Was the application associated with differences in direct medical costs for patients or families?

Was the application associated with differences for patients or families in other direct costs (e.g., travel, child care) or indirect cost (e.g., lost work days)?

What were the costs for society overall compared to the alternative(s)?

Was an application associated with differences in total health care costs, the cost per service, per episode of illness, or per capita?

How did the costs of the application relate to the benefits of the telemedicine application compared to the alternative(s)?

Evaluating Patient Perceptions

Were patients satisfied with the telemedicine service compared to the alternative(s)?

How did patients rate their physical and psychological comfort with the application?

How did patients rate the convenience of the encounter, its duration, its timeliness, and its cost?

How did patients (and family members) rate the skills and personal manner of the consultant and the attending personnel (e.g., primary care physician, nurse practitioner)?

Was the lack of direct physical contact with the distant clinician acceptable?

How did patients rate the explanations provided to them of what their problem was and what was being recommended?

Did patients have concerns about whether the privacy of personal medical information was protected?

Would patients be willing to use the telemedicine service again?

Overall, how satisfied were patients with the telemedicine services they received?

Evaluating Clinician Perceptions

Were attending/consulting clinicians satisfied with the telemedicine application compared to the alternative(s)?

How did attending/consulting clinicians rate their comfort with telemedicine equipment and procedures?

How did attending/consulting clinicians rate the convenience of telemedicine in terms of scheduling, physical arrangements, and location?

How did attending/consulting clinicians rate the timeliness of consultation results?

How did attending/consulting clinicians rate the technical quality of the service?

How did attending/consulting clinicians rate the quality of communications with patients?

Were attending/consulting clinicians concerned about maintaining the confidentiality of personal medical information and protecting patients' privacy?

Did attending/consulting clinicians believe the application made a positive contribution to patient care?

Would the clinicians be willing to use the telemedicine services again?

Overall, how satisfied were the attending/consulting clinicians with the telemedicine service?

1

Introduction and Background

For more than 30 years, clinicians, health services researchers, and others have been investigating the use of advanced telecommunications and computer technologies to improve health care. At the intersection of many of these efforts is telemedicine—a combination of mainstream and innovative information technologies. As defined here, telemedicine is *the use of electronic information and communications technologies to provide and support health care when distance separates the participants.*

On the commonplace side of the spectrum are familiar uses of the telephone for consultations between patients and clinicians and the use of radio to link emergency medical personnel to medical centers. On the other end of the telemedicine spectrum are largely experimental innovations such as telesurgery in which a surgeon receives visual and tactile information to guide robotic instruments to perform surgery at a distant site. In between these two ends of the spectrum lie an array of video, audio, and data transmission technologies and applications. Some, such as relatively expensive interactive video conferencing, allow clinicians to see, hear, examine, question, and counsel distant patients for "real-time" diagnostic and therapeutic purposes. Others, based on "store and forward" technologies, permit digital images and other information to be saved and transmitted relatively cheaply to consultants who can receive